This book belongs to
someone daring...
someone who isn't afraid to speak
her mind and make her own way...
someone who is a smart, capable,
and courageous girl...

Tasha Hilborn

(your name here)

Happy 13ᵀᴴ
Birthday

Love, Grandma.

Titles by Ashley Rice
Published by
Blue Mountain Arts®

For an Incredible Kid
Girl Power
Girls Rule
Sisters Are Forever Friends
You Are a Girl Who Can Do Anything
You Are a Girl Who Totally Rocks!
You Go, Girl... Keep Dreaming

For an Incredible Girl/Para una niña increíble
(Bilingual Edition)

Library of Congress Control Number: 2013939962
ISBN: 978-1-59842-760-8

Blue Mountain Press is registered in U.S. Patent and Trademark Office.
Certain trademarks are used under license.

Printed in China.
First Printing: 2013

Blue Mountain Arts, Inc.
P.O. Box 4549, Boulder, Colorado 80306

You Are a Girl Who Can Do Anything

...a very special book
to cheer you on
and help you
achieve greatness

Ashley Rice

Blue Mountain Press ™

Boulder, Colorado

You Are a Girl Who Can Do Anything

Follow your dreams, wherever they might take you. Find things that you enjoy doing and good friends with good hearts. Be yourself and believe in yourself and don't take anything for granted. As you grow up, don't be afraid to stumble. Know that you can learn and grow from each experience.

Listen carefully to your heart. Stand tall and proud, and know that there is greatness out there — you just have to trust in yourself to find it.

You Have Everything It Takes to Succeed

Stay positive no matter what.
Life never gives us more
than we can handle,
and you are more than up to the task
of facing every challenge.
You've got a brilliance
that outshines any star.
Never forget who you are,
what you stand for,
or what you've been through before.
All these things
will strengthen your spirit
and help you out
as you make your way
into new adventures
and stand up to adversities.

There is nothing that
you can't overcome
with a little bit of courage.
You are a unique
and talented individual
who has everything it takes
to succeed in this life.

You Are a Girl
Who Will Go Far

You know where you're going,
and you've got a good head
on your shoulders.
You make good decisions,
and you surround yourself
with positive people.
You excel in work and in play,
and you are not afraid
to have a little fun every once in a while.
You set goals and you reach them,
all the while remembering
those around you
and attending to their needs.
You are unselfish,
but you always remember
to take care of yourself —
indulging in little things
when the mood strikes you.

You are capable
and honest and practical,
but you are also passionate
about what you do
and who you are.
You are giving and loving
and independent.
You know what you want
and how to get it,
and you do not hesitate
to take chances
in order to reach your dreams.
You are a realist and an idealist,
and you care about
what happens to people.
You are kind and
understanding and unique.
You are a girl who will go far.

Reach for the Stars and You Will Catch Them

There's a light inside you
that is brighter than sunshine.
There's a hope inside you
that can get you through anything.
There's a strength inside you
that is so great.
No matter what happens,
just know that you are
up to the challenges
that life places before you.

Know that nothing is
too good for you.
You deserve the best
life has to offer,
and it is all within your reach.
All you have to do is
put yourself out there,
give it everything you've got,
and reach for the stars.
You will catch them
if you only believe in yourself.

Be the Best
You Ever

The best you can do is to be your
true self. If you are true to yourself,
others will be attracted to you.
You'll have a spring in your step and
a grin on your face that will send
people running your way. You are an
amazing person to begin with, and if
you are true to who you are, there
is no telling what you can accomplish.

The possibilities are limitless,
and the world is open to you
every day. Look to your own
heart to show you what to do.
Only then can you be the best
version of yourself!

Being true to yourself takes guts. First, you've got to face everything around you and figure out what is important: what you think really counts. Second, you've got to interact with a lot of people who may see things differently. But life has lots of smiles and frowns, as days have their own ups and downs.

And if you are true to yourself
in all that you do, and if you keep
working to make your dreams
come true, then you will achieve
success just by doing your best.

You've got everything it takes to
be true to you.

♥

♥　　♥

It's a Girl's World

It's a girl's world
where anything is possible.
Believe in your dreams,
because they are what
allow the future to unfold,
and the future is just
waiting for you
to make it everything
you can!

It's a girl's world
where tomorrow is a rainbow
for you to slide down.
Reach for the stars,
and find happiness
in the everyday moments
that make up your week.

It's a girl's world,
so start dreaming now.
You never know
where you might go!

How Will You Make Your Mark?

Think of all the great girls who came before you. What motivated them? What made them shine? You are one of those great girls, and you are following in their footsteps — lighting the way for others who will come after you. You are an amazing girl with grace and talent and wit and understanding. What you do now will influence generations of girls to come. So what will you do? How will you make your mark?

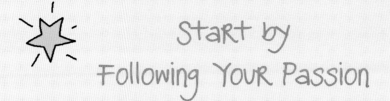

Start by
Following Your Passion

Find something that you are passionate about and stick with it. No matter what anybody else says, pursue what you love. Have faith in yourself when times are hard and it seems like there is no end in sight. Follow your passion wherever it takes you.

Your passion will be there for you — lighting the way and keeping you inspired and on your toes. It will give you a reason to get up in the morning and to believe in the stars. Your passion may keep you up some nights, but it's worth it to find something you believe in that much.

YOUR Destiny Is in YOUR Own Hands

Don't expect other people
to make you happy.
YOUR destiny is in YOUR own hands,
and it is up to you to make the best
that you can of YOUR life every day.
Depend on yourself
to make things happen for you.
Don't wait around for things to go YOUR way
or for fate to change YOUR life.
Instead, walk into the ball game,
grab the bat, and hit a home run.

People will say that
you can't get it done.
But don't listen to them!
Only you know what
you are really capable of.
Only you know the distance
you are willing to go.
So trust in your heart
and believe with
everything you are
that you can get
where you are going.
Great things await
if you have the determination
to see them through!

Show the World
What You've Got

You have so much to offer.
All you've got to do
is get out there
and show them what you've got.
Put your best foot forward
and be everything you can be.
Don't be afraid to trust yourself.
Your true self is the only one
who will see you through
to brighter days.

You've got a spirit
that outshines the sun
and sparkles more
than the greatest stars.
You can climb any mountain
and see your way through
any path that is set before you.
You are incredible,
and you are only getting better
every single day.

You Are Brave, Amazing, and Real

You know what you want,
and you don't give up.

You are understanding,
and you know how to be a true friend.
You are a superstar.
You are sensitive to those around you,
and you are always trying to make
people feel more comfortable.
You constantly reach out to others
by lending a helping hand or offering a smile
to those in need of a pick-me-up.

You know that
we all make mistakes,
and you are willing
to overlook other people's flaws.
You are always ready
to offer help
to someone who needs it.
You are one of a kind,
and there is no one else like you.

There's something extra special
about you that makes you
different from the rest.
You've got the strength of heart
that you need to pass life's tests.
You're beautiful and amazing
and unique in your own way.
You've got what it takes
to get through the days.

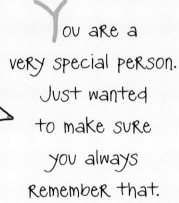

You are a
very special person.
Just wanted
to make sure
you always
Remember that.

When You Persevere, Anything Can Happen

Persevere when you can't see the next turn in the road. Persevere when you are at your wits' end and you're not sure if you can make it.

Don't give up when the path is all uphill and you are out of breath and want to quit. Keep going when night is upon you and you are waiting for the break of dawn. When it seems like you have nothing left to give, know that you <u>can</u> make it.

Be strong when others around you
are falling down. Keep an angel in
your pocket for the times when
you are stressed. Hold on to hope
like a bright balloon in the breeze.
Court courage like there is no
tomorrow. Believe that good things
can happen, and they will.

Keep Your chin Up!

Keep your chin up
when storm clouds surround you and
you wonder what'll happen next.
Always remember you can overcome
whatever comes your way.
Keep your chin up
when those around you
go astray.
Know that you can
climb mountains
in your own way.

Keep your chin up
when you aren't sure
which way to go.
Deep inside you,
you already know.
Keep your chin up
no matter what's
going on in your life.
You can do anything
you put your mind to.

It's Okay to Fail Sometimes

If you never try,
you will never know
whether you can succeed.
Life is about making mistakes,
learning from them,
and moving forward
into the future.
So go ahead and fail.
Fail and fail again —
and you will realize
that from your failures
come the greatest successes
you could ever imagine.

Take a step and then
take another.
If you fall, get up again
and keep on going.
It is only by taking these steps
that you can get anywhere at all.
And where you are going
is a magnificent place.
All you have to do
is get started!

Look Deep Inside for the Courage You Need

You know you can do it!
You've overcome
similar obstacles before
and made your way
with a smile on your face
and hope to spare.
You can accomplish so much,
and you are more than prepared
to face today with open arms.

Know that your dreams
are very special
and mean a lot.
Know that great things
are coming to you.
All you have to do
is accept them
and give this day
and every day
everything you've got!

Remember...
You Are Not Alone

You are going through
an important and exciting
time in your life!
You are developing physically
and emotionally,
and you are probably going
to experience a lot of changes.
It's important to remember
that you are not alone
in the challenges you face.

Rely on your parents and friends
when you have problems
that you need to address.
They are there for you
and want to help you
get through this amazing
stage in your life.
Always remember that
you've got people on your side
to help you out along the way.

Good Friends Are So Important to Have

Good friends are there for
each other when no one else is.
They stand by each other
through good times and bad —
always ready to offer up a smile
even in the most trying situations.
Good friends listen to each other
and lean on each other
on the long road that is life.

Good friends are always around
to share secrets with,
to laugh with,
and to encourage each other
along the way.
They are the shining stars —
the beacons by which
we find our way home.
Good friends trust each other
and rely on each other.
Good friends hold a very special
place in our lives and our hearts,
and we are oh so lucky
to have them to talk to every day.

The Little Things
Can Make a Big Difference

Never let your destination get in the way
of your journey of self-discovery. Life is to
be savored and enjoyed. Revel in each moment
of every day. Take time for yourself — time
to take a walk, smell the roses, and feel the
wind in the trees. You are your own mapmaker,
your own compass.

Notice everything around you, and let it all make
you grin. Open your heart to new opportunities
and believe that they will be exciting and bring
good fortune your way. Let the sunshine warm
your skin and bathe you in its promise of
happiness. Appreciate everything you've got.
Keep promises to yourself about your dreams
and know that they can come true in every way!

Set goals, but make sure to leave space for the little things in life — the milestones, the celebrations, and the moments spent with people you love. You will reach your dreams, but you will also look back on your life and feel happy that you enjoyed everything around you. These memories are worth saving and will be etched in your mind forever.

Focus on the Here and Now

Don't let worries about
the future get you down.
Everything you need
to be happy is in your own hands.
Just stay positive,
look on the bright side
of everything,
and don't let anything
stand in the way
of enjoying this moment.

All we have is "Right now."
We don't know what
the future will bring,
and the past is the past —
it's something that once happened
but is over now
and can't affect us anymore.
Keep your memories with you,
but forge on into today.
It's a great place to be!

Each Day Is a Chance for You To...

 try new things

 see what tomorrow brings

 look for rainbows
and walk in the sunshine

 take a step forward
and say what's on your mind

 find beauty in each
and every little thing

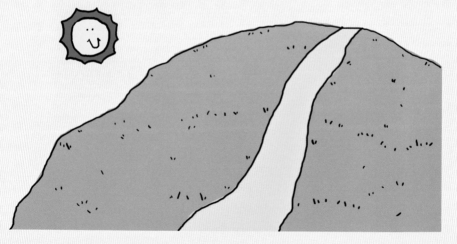

open up your heart
to what the future holds

 be yourself

 find your own way

 make the world a better place

 have fun!

Expect Great Things to Happen, and They Will

Set the stage for your dreams to come true by having positive thoughts and sending positive energy out into the world. The world responds to positivity, and it will soon open its doors to you if you only have the right attitude. Think about things going your way, and then they <u>will</u> start to go your way.

Of course, you've got to put in the work. You've got to show up every day and give it your best shot.
But if you do this, if you are your best self and think only your best thoughts, there is nothing that can stop you from achieving your goals and more.

Look to Your Heart for Answers

When you don't know
which way to turn,
look to your heart to show you
which way to go.
Your heart knows the answers
to everything you've been
dreaming about,
and it will take you
to those dreams
and make your soul
smile big.
Even when the road is tough,
you've got all the answers
you need to know.

You've got all the confidence it takes
to go all the way to the top!
Just look to your hopes and dreams,
and they will be enough
to get you to a brand-new day.
Soon you will be
singing in the rain
and dancing on rainbows.

DO YOUR BEST

You don't have to be perfect. People don't expect you to be, and you shouldn't expect yourself to be either! Life is a bumpy road, and it is sometimes during our mistakes and "failings" that we make our greatest discoveries. So just do your best.

If you hit some pitfalls, take a breath
and tell yourself that everything is
going to be okay. And it will be! It may
take a lot of detours to get where
you are going, but those detours
are all worth it, every one. You never
know what you might find when you
are making one of your "mistakes."
It just might lead you on the road to
something wonderful and beyond your
greatest hopes. Just be yourself and
let life happen, and you will be better
than fine... you will be amazing!

You'll Get There...
One Step at a Time

Always think of the good
that can come out of any situation.
Try to see that life's hurdles
always have a bright side.
They make us stronger
and better versions of ourselves.
They push us to be our best
at all times and to always
have a positive outlook.
Hard times challenge us
to find the best way to go
and the most healthy way
to deal with anything
that comes our way.

If you can get through life
one step at a time,
you will find that you can
handle whatever happens.
Just take the days as they come,
and don't become overwhelmed
by small things that seem
to stand in your way.
Instead, show <u>them</u> who's boss.
Take initiative in your own life,
and you will be astonished
at the greatness that awaits you.

Everything's Going to Turn Out Fine

Sometimes life puts
a hurdle in your path
that seems hard
to jump over.

That's when it's time
to dig deep, look within,
and find the courage
and determination
to face your challenges.
Look to yourself for answers,
and never give up the fight.
Know that you have
strength within.
You will get through this
and everything else,
and you will come out
an even better person for it!

You Always Have an Angel Looking Out for You

When you're down,
an angel is there
to share your troubles
and lend a guiding hand.
This angel adds a silver lining
to your roughest days.
When you're happy,
your angel celebrates
your successes and
showers you with stars.

Wherever you go
and whatever you do,
this angel is looking
out for you the whole time.
No matter what happens to you,
don't get too worried.
Your angel is with you
every step of the way,
making sure that everything
will turn out okay.
When you've got an angel
looking out for you,
you are blessed.

Your Life Is a Storybook

You are a girl
who leads the way for others.
You are a girl
who is beautiful
and amazing.
You make a brighter day
for those around you,
and you light up a room
with your smile.

Once upon a time...

...and she lived happily
ever after.

You are a girl
who makes her way
with strength, humor, and love.
You never give up,
and you are always willing
to go the extra mile.
You are a girl
who is fearless
and able to face anything.
You are a girl
whose life is a storybook,
and you are the heroine.

May All Your Wishes Come True

May you have fun doing all the things you love to do. May you have a smile on your face every day. May you be loved and cared for. May you get to see your friends and laugh with them. May you get closer to achieving your dreams. May hope smile at your door. May you be surrounded by your family. May things work out the way you want them to. May you have a happy life.

May you dance and grin and
laugh and spin around a lot in
your heart. May you win many
times (and be proud of yourself)
and — no matter what — always
trust yourself. May you follow
your heart and always remain as
strong as you are now, today.

Dare to Be Great!

Dreaming is the greatest gift
you can give yourself.
But if you don't turn those
dreams into actions,
you are cheating yourself
out of one of life's true pleasures.
Imagine all the things
that you can do
and all the places
that you can go in your life.
Imagine that the world
is at your fingertips
and all you have to do
is say the word.
Don't just dream it;
do it!

Dare to be great.
Dare to go out there
and show the world
everything you can do.
Dare to dream big
and to follow all the possibilities
life holds for you.
Dare to be the person
that you are.
Dare to take a step
in the right direction
and keep going.

Dare to do
whatever you can
to make your life
the best it can be.